Wild Britain

Barn Owl

Louise and Richard Spilsbury

H www.heinemann.co.uk
Visit our website to find out more information about Heinemann Library books.

To order:
☎ Phone 44 (0) 1865 888066
📄 Send a fax to 44 (0) 1865 314091
💻 Visit the Heinemann Bookshop at www.heinemann.co.uk to browse our catalogue and order online.

First published in Great Britain by Heinemann Library, Halley Court, Jordan Hill, Oxford OX2 8EJ, part of Harcourt Education Ltd. Heinemann is a registered trademark of Harcourt Education Ltd.

Editorial: Lucy Thunder and Helen Cannons
Design: David Poole and Celia Floyd
Illustrations: Jeff Edwards, Alan Fraser and Geoff Ward
Picture Research: Rebecca Sodergren and Peter Morris
Production: Edward Moore

Originated by Repro Multi-Warna
Printed and bound in China by South China Printing Company

The paper used to print this book comes from sustainable resources.

ISBN 0 431 03981 X (hardback)
08 07 06 05 04
10 9 8 7 6 5 4 3 2 1

ISBN 0 431 03988 7 (paperback)
09 08 07 06 05
10 9 8 7 6 5 4 3 2 1

British Library Cataloguing in Publication Data
Spilsbury, Louise and Spilsbury, Richard
Barn owl. – (Wild britain)
598.9'7

A full catalogue record for this book is available from the British Library.

Acknowledgements

The Publishers would like to thank the following for permission to reproduce photographs:

Ardea p4; Ardea/Piers Cavendish p24; Ardea/John Daniels p6; Bruce Coleman/Jane Burton pp18, 20; Bruce Coleman/Kim Taylor pp5, 25; Corbis/Darrell Gulin p14; FLPA/Ray Bird p27; FLPA/Michael Callan pp19, 21; FLPA/David Hosking pp11, 28; FLPA/E. & D. Hosking p15; FLPA/Martin Withers p23; Nature Picture Library p16; NHPA/Stephen Dalton pp12, 13; NHPA/Michael Leach p17; NHPA/Andy Rouse p10; NHPA/Allan Williams p29; Oxford Scientific Films p9; Oxford Scientific Films/Larry Crowhurst p8; Oxford Scientific Films/Michael Leach p26; Windrush Photos p22.

Cover photograph of a barn owl resting, reproduced with permission of Ardea/Chris Knights.

The Publishers would like to thank Michael Scott for his assistance in the preparation of this book.

Every effort has been made to contact copyright holders of any material reproduced in this book. Any omissions will be rectified in subsequent printings if notice is given to the Publisher.

Contents

Any words appearing in the text in bold, **like this**, are explained in the Glossary.

What are barn owls?

Barn owls have heart-shaped faces with black shiny eyes and small sharp beaks.

Barn owls are beautiful birds that live in Britain. A barn owl has white **feathers** on its face and belly. It has pale orange-gold feathers on its back and on top of its **wings**.

Can you tell which is the male and which is the female barn owl in this picture?

Male barn owls are usually a slightly lighter colour than **females**. Female barn owls usually have black spots on their belly.

Where do barn owls live?

Barn owls got their name because they like to live in barns!

Barn owls mostly live in farmland areas.
They like to fly over open stretches of
land, and shelter in barns and other
farm buildings.

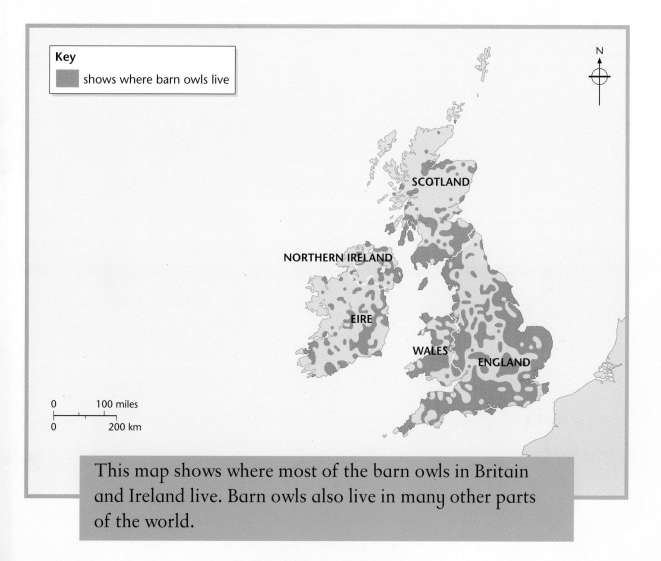

This map shows where most of the barn owls in Britain and Ireland live. Barn owls also live in many other parts of the world.

Barn owls also live in open land where there are small groups of trees near by. They do not like to live in forests with many trees close together.

What do barn owls eat?

Barn owls swallow small animals whole.

Barn owls often eat small animals, such as **voles** and mice. Sometimes they eat frogs, rats, small birds and young rabbits.

You can tell what a barn owl has been eating from looking at pellets like this.

Barn owls eat animal meat, but not bones, **feathers** or fur. They squash these things into a **pellet** while in their stomach. Then they spit the pellets out.

Finding food

Barn owls have excellent hearing to help them catch small animals in the dark.

Barn owls mainly **hunt** for food at night or in the early evening. They listen carefully to hear a small animal moving. Then they catch it in their sharp **talons**.

This barn owl is looking round to see what made a sound. Could it be something to eat?

Barn owls have big eyes so they can see well in the dark. They can turn their head right round to look in any direction.

On the move

Barn owls fly silently so they can hear the animals they want to catch and eat.

Barn owls have long, wide **wings**. The **feathers** on their wings are very soft. Their wings make very little noise when they fly.

This barn owl is dropping down to catch a rat. The owl may run along the ground after the rat if it misses.

When barn owls **hunt**, they fly close to the ground. When they drop down to catch food, they hold their wings back and stretch out their legs.

Resting and sleeping

Barn owls like to rest and sleep in quiet places like tree holes. They live alone or in pairs.

Barn owls rest or sleep during the day. They usually sleep in holes in trees or in the roof of a barn. They sometimes sleep in caves or wells!

Barn owls, like other birds, clean their feathers to keep them healthy.

The pattern of a barn owl's back **feathers** helps to keep it safe when it rests. The colours and patterns blend in against **bark** and in fields to hide it.

Barn owl eggs

These barn owl eggs are on a ledge in a barn.

Barn owls **lay** their **eggs** in a hollow in a tree or in an old building, such as a barn. They do not build **nests** to lay their eggs in. They lay them on ledges or in holes.

This female barn owl is sitting on her eggs.

The **female** barn owl usually lays four to six eggs in April. The eggs are white. She sits on the eggs to keep them warm. This helps the baby owls inside to grow.

Young barn owls

This baby owl is just breaking out of its egg. A baby owl is called a chick.

The **female** sits on the **eggs** for a month. Then they start to **hatch**. The female stays with her baby owls for about three weeks.

Barn owls use their beaks to tear food up for their chicks.

The **male** barn owl brings food to his family. He carries it to them in his **talons**. The female tears the food up into pieces so the **chicks** can eat it.

Growing up

These young owls are waiting for their parents to bring them food.

When the **chicks** are three weeks old they can swallow whole **voles** and mice. Their mother sleeps somewhere else now. She helps the father to find food for the chicks.

When young barn owls can fly, they begin to catch their own food.

The young owls can fly when they are about two months old. Now they are ready to leave their parents. They fly away to find somewhere to live near by.

Barn owl sounds

When it is time to lay eggs, **male** barn owls call to **females** with lots of twittering sounds.

Barn owls do not hoot, but they make lots of other sounds. They scream, click, hiss and even snore!

Young barn owls often make a wheezing, snoring noise to ask a parent for food.

Barn owls sitting on **eggs** hiss if something surprises them. When adult barn owls return to their **chicks** they often make a croaking sound to say hello!

Under attack

Peregrine Falcons are large birds of prey that sometimes catch barn owls.

There are not many wild animals that **hunt** barn owls. Sometimes large **birds of prey** catch and eat barn owls.

Barn owls and their eggs are protected by law.

Barn owls are protected wild birds. This means it is against the law for anyone to hurt them. People are **fined** a lot of money if they disturb or take barn owl **eggs**.

Dangers

Some barn owls are killed by cars on roads.

Barn owls sometimes fly near to roads to catch small animals that live near by. Sometimes the owls are killed by cars. Most wild barn owls live to be around five years old.

Many barns are being turned into houses. That means there are fewer places for barn owls to rest and **lay** their **eggs**.

Today many farmers have large, tidy fields, with few rough grassy areas. That means there are fewer small animals for owls to **hunt**. Barn owls are becoming quite **rare**.

A barn owl's year

This barn owl is carrying food in its **talons** to feed to his babies.

Baby barn owls **hatch** in late spring, when lots of animals have babies. That means there are a lot of small animals for barn owls to feed to their **chicks**.

In winter, barn owls may have to hunt during the day and night to catch enough food.

It is harder for barn owls to **hunt** for food in winter. Barn owls are light and cannot fly in strong winds. The small animals that they eat may also stay hidden more.

Owls in Britain

As well as the barn owl, there are several other kinds of owl in Britain. Here are three of them. What differences can you see between these owls and the barn owl?

tawny owl

long-eared owl

little owl

The artwork on this page is not to scale.

Glossary

bark hard outer covering around a tree

birds of prey large, strong birds that hunt and catch other animals for food

chick young bird that is not yet fully grown and able to fly

eggs young of some animals grow inside eggs until they hatch out

feathers most of a bird's body is covered in feathers. Feathers keep a bird warm and help it to fly.

female animal that can become a mother when it is grown up. A female human is called a woman or a girl.

fined to have to pay money as a punishment

hatch born from an egg

hunt to find and catch other animals to eat

lay when an egg comes out of an animal's body

male animal that can become a father when it is grown up. A male human is called a man or a boy.

nest something a bird makes to lay its eggs in

pellet package of bones and fur that barn owls cough up because they cannot eat them

rare when there is only a small number of something

talons long sharp claws on a bird's feet

vole small mouse-like animal

wings feathered 'arms' on each side of a bird's body

Index